COLORING WITH ME

TRUE LOVE COLORING BOOK

VALENTINE'S DAY COLORING BOOK

M. R. KAYE

We Love Valentine's Day

BLANK PAGE #1 - CUT OUT

This page has been provided so that you can place it between your working coloring page and the one underneath. This will assist with protecting your other pages from indentations and ink bleeding through.

BLANK PAGE #2 - CUT OUT

This page has been provided so that you can place it between your working coloring page and the one underneath. This will assist with protecting your other pages from indentations and ink bleeding through.

ABOUT THE AUTHOR

M.R Kaye writes and lives in Western Montana. A lover of nature and animals, and all that is curious, creative and artful in the world.   With a series of Did You Know? Books, coloring books and other projects under way, M. R. hopes to instill questioning into the life of a child and bring back the childlike joy of coloring for adults.

In these changing and challenging times, I hope to also help people find hope and beauty through the process of coloring and learning about the world around them

Inquiry leads to intelligence, or at least it leads to a life of learning. while continued creativity through outlets like coloring lead to an engaged brain later in life.I hope my books will be enjoyed by kids of all ages for years to come. I hope that they will learn, and in learning, desire to learn even more.

My wish is that you will make learning a joyful lifelong pursuit.

ColoringWithMe.com

A SIMPLE REQUEST FROM THE AUTHOR

I hope you enjoyed your experience Coloring With Me.

If you did I have just one tiny favor to ask that would mean a lot to me and also to other folks looking to get this book.

If you are able to take just a minute to leave us a review of your experience, it would mean so very much to me.

It can be as long or as short as you wish to make it. If you would like to share a picture of something you colored from the book, please do.

Thanks so very much for Coloring With Me.

M. R. Kaye.

Other Great Books In Our Coloring With Me Series

Find Our Books on

Amazon our Author Page is M. R. Kaye

Etsy our Shop is called Montana Diva Creations

Always Check Amazon For MORE Titles and visit Coloringwithme.com

Made in the USA
Las Vegas, NV
27 July 2022